Contents

KW-263-132

People around the world belong to different groups. You are part of a family, a school and maybe a club or team, too. People also come from different countries and religions. Most of the time different groups live side by side and in peace.

4

People don't always get along though. When they don't, they come into conflict. They may fight or try to hurt each other. When we see news about conflicts around the world it can make us feel sad, angry and scared. This book will help you make sense of what's happening.

When people argue, they usually sort out their problem
fairly quickly, but conflicts happen when groups of
people or countries cannot solve their problems
by talking, and they start fighting. Conflicts
may happen when one group or country tries
to take land from another. Or people fight
to stop others being hurt or treated badly.

Some people think that everyone should live the same way they do. They may try to get other people to share their beliefs and customs. If they try to force other people to follow their rules, this can also cause conflict and violence.

During a war, different groups battle with each other until one side gives up or loses. Sometimes the war stops because they've been able to talk through their problems. Leaders decide how, where and when to fight their enemy. Soldiers attack each other using weapons and bombs. People from both sides who do not fight in the war are called civilians.

Most people believe that war is bad and that it is better to sort out problems by talking. But people sometimes go to war because they think that it is the only way to stop bad things from happening. Soldiers who fight in wars do so to protect the things and people that they care about.

Terrorism is when people carry out acts of violence to get attention for their ideas and aims. Terrorists hide and set off bombs in places such as airports and train stations. Religious groups carry out some terrorist attacks because they feel badly treated or disagree with other people's beliefs.

Terrorists want to scare people so that world leaders do what they want. But it's important to remember that the chances a terrorist will hurt you or the people you love are very, very small.

People on both sides of a conflict can be injured or killed in war and terrorist attacks. Homes and belongings may be ruined during fighting. The places where people work, worship or study may be burned down.

Sometimes people leave their homes to escape terrible fighting or violence. They go to find a safer place to live and a better life. People who leave their home country because their lives are in danger are called refugees.

Conflicts can change people's lives forever. People have to find new homes and mend roads, bridges and buildings. Refugees have to find somewhere new to live and work. They also have to make new friends and often learn a new language. After a conflict, people may feel scared and sad for a long time.

Imagine not being able to go to school. When schools are destroyed, children lose the chance to learn and play together. So, teachers may give classes in unusual places until a new school is built.

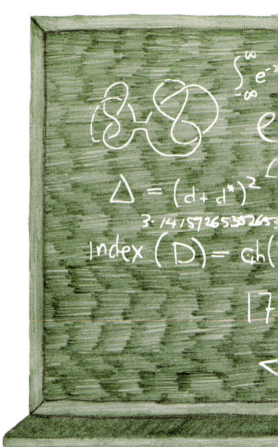

A charity is a group that helps people in need. Charity workers bring clean water, food, blankets and tents to people who have lost their homes. They comfort people who are upset. They bring doctors, nurses and medicines to help people who are hurt.

Governments and charity workers also help people get their lives back to normal. They find homes for refugees to live in. They also pay for the materials people need to make new buildings, mend power lines and bring them tools and machines so people can start work again.

Rules keep us safe. At school there are rules to stop people hitting or bullying other people. The world has a set of rules about what happens in war. These rules protect children, civilians, injured soldiers, hospitals and the places where people go to worship.

Most people obey these laws during a war. If they do not, they can be punished. They may be put in prison for their crimes. Other countries may stop buying and selling things from a country that breaks war laws. This can make a country obey the laws again.

It's good if you can sort out arguments on your own, but sometimes you may need an adult's help. There are people who help to sort out world conflicts, too. The United Nations is a group of countries that work together to end wars and protects civilians.

The United Nations and world leaders try to get the two sides in a war to talk. They help different groups to find a fair way to sort out their problems, without hurting each other, or other people. They try to solve the problems with words not weapons.

It is normal for people to disagree sometimes. The important thing is not to let an argument turn into a fight. It helps if people can stay calm and say what they think in a polite, friendly way. If people shout and say mean things, both sides can lose their temper.

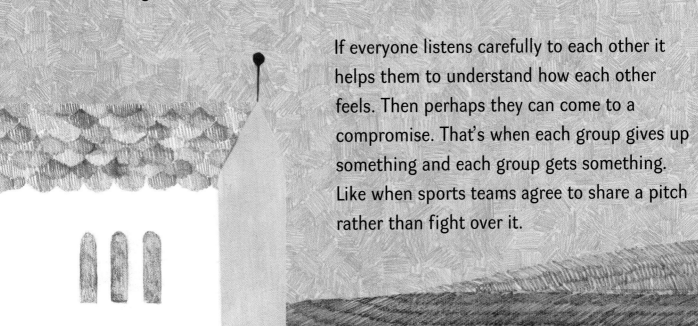

If everyone listens carefully to each other it helps them to understand how each other feels. Then perhaps they can come to a compromise. That's when each group gives up something and each group gets something. Like when sports teams agree to share a pitch rather than fight over it.

One way to avoid conflicts is to understand each other better. We are all the same in lots of ways. We all need a home, food, water, family and friends. We all deserve to be safe and choose our own beliefs. Understanding others helps us to show respect to live together in peace.

It is natural to feel angry when we see people being hurt. But we shouldn't blame a whole group of people when a few people do something wrong. If one pupil stole a computer from your school, it would be wrong to say that all of the children in your school were thieves, wouldn't it?

It's good to learn and care about world conflicts, but it's bad to worry about them too much. If you are upset, talk to an adult you trust about how you feel. They can help you. It also helps to think about what's good in the world and to do things that you enjoy, like playing with friends.

Most people are caring and kind. The main reason we see conflicts in the news is that they don't happen very often. You and your family are not at great risk of danger. Remember: there are lots of clever people working to stop wars and terrorism, and to make the world a safer place for us all.

It feels good to help people. There are lots of things you could do. You could collect food or clothes to give refugees. You could bake cakes or put on a show to raise money for charities that help people in conflicts. Or write a letter to the government asking them to help. What ideas do you have?

Find Out More

Books

Seeking Refuge: Ali's Story – A Journey from Afghanistan
Andy Glynne, Wayland, 2015

Seeking Refuge: Navid's Story – A Journey from Iran
Andy Glynne, Wayland, 2016

Who are Refugees and Migrants? What Makes
People Leave their Homes? And Other Big Questions.
Michael Rosen and Annemarie Young, Wayland, 2016

Websites

Save the Children works to protect children in
need all over the world.
www.savethechildren.org.uk

The Red Cross is a charity that helps victims
of war and disaster.
www.redcross.org.uk

Glossary

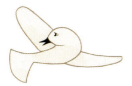

charity a group that helps people in need

civilian a person who is not in the army

compromise when two sides both give up something to come to an agreement

conflict a very angry disagreement, fight, battle or war

custom something that a group of people regularly does together

government group of people who control and make decisions for a country

refugee person who leaves their home country because it's not safe anymore to find a safer place to live

religion a belief in a god or gods, for example Islam and Christianity

respect to care about other people's feelings and opinions

terrorist a person who uses bombs and other violent acts to scare people

United Nations a group of countries that work together to prevent and end wars

worship to show respect for a god, for example by praying

Index